LIFESKILLS IN ACTION

JOB SKILLS

D0981136

Job Interview Basics

M.G. HIGGINS

LIFESKILLS IN ACTION

JOB SKILLS

MONEY	Living on a Budget | Road Trip
	Opening a Bank Account | The Guitar
	Managing Credit | High Cost
	Using Coupons | Get the Deal
	Planning to Save | Something Big
LIVING	Smart Grocery Shopping | Shop Smart
	Doing Household Chores | Keep It Clean
	Finding a Place to Live | A Place of Our Own
	Moving In | Pack Up
	Cooking Your Own Meals | Dinner Is Served
JOB	Preparing a Resume | Not Her Job
	Finding a Job | Dream Jobs
	Job Interview Basics| Job Ready
	How to Act Right on the Job| Choices
	Employee Rights| Not So Sweet

SADDLEBACK
EDUCATIONAL PUBLISHING
www.sdlback.com

Copyright © 2017 by Saddleback Educational Publishing. All rights reserved. No part of this book may be reproduced in any form or by any means, electronic or mechanical, including photocopying, recording, scanning, or by any information storage and retrieval system, without the written permission of the publisher. SADDLEBACK EDUCATIONAL PUBLISHING and any associated logos are trademarks and/or registered trademarks of Saddleback Educational Publishing.

ISBN: 978-1-68021-410-9
eBook: 978-1-63078-811-7

Printed in Malaysia

24 23 22 21 20   3 4 5 6 7

Getting a job is a process.

Companies get many applications.

They pick ones they like.

Then they want to know more.

That is where an **interview** comes in.

It is your chance to shine.

INTERVIEW

Someone contacts you.

They want to set up an interview.

This is a meeting.

It's a way to get to know you.

The employer asks questions.

Be ready to answer.

Help them see why you are a **good fit**.

An interview may be with one person.

It could be with a group.

Most take place **at the business**.

Some are by phone.

Others are online.

Sometimes there is more than one interview.

There may be many people to meet with.

Meetings may happen on different days.

Interviews can be short.

Many take an hour.

Some may be even longer.

It depends on the job.

An interview is scheduled.

Take time to get ready.

Some companies interview many people for a job.

Make sure you stand out.

Being prepared is key.

Read the job ad again.

The company wants certain skills.

Do you have them?

They will ask.

Think about how to answer the questions.

Show that you can **meet their needs**.

Web Content Manager

Workplace

Necess

Learn about the business.

Look them up online.

Know what the company does.

Maybe they make products.

They could provide a service.

Read about the people.

The owners might be listed.

Other leaders could be noted.

Find out everything you can.

This will help you in the interview.

Think about **possible questions**.

Some will be simple.

They help people get to know you.

Others will dig deeper.

These look for what kind of worker you are.

NO...
DATE ....

- Tell me about you.

- How much do you know about our company?

- What are your strengths?

- What are your weaknesses?

- Why do you want to work here?

- Where do you see yourself in five years?

- Why should we hire you?

These are just a few.

Find others online.

There are many lists of questions.

It helps to be ready to answer.

Practice answering aloud.

Have someone ask each question.

Answer like you're in the interview.

Preparing is smart.

SEARCH ENGINE

Answers should be **true**.

Stick to the topic.

Don't ramble.

Be specific.

Think of a project you led.

You may have finished a big task.

Maybe you solved a tough problem.

Tell a brief story.

This might be from a job.

It could be from school.

They will ask if you have questions.

Don't say no.

Have at least one in mind.

It shows you care.

You are serious about the job.

Don't ask about pay or vacation.

Talk about details later.

Wait until you have a job offer.

The day of the interview comes.

Make sure you are **neat and clean**.

Take a shower.

Shave.

Brush your teeth.

Comb your hair.

Trim your nails.

Cover tattoos.

Some places won't want to see them.

Be careful about scents.

Think about what to wear.

Dress well.

Some people wear a suit.

Others wear nice pants and a shirt.

They might wear a skirt and a blouse.

Make sure clothes fit well.

Take everything you need.

Bring copies of your **resume**.

Have a notebook and pen.

Make notes if you need to.

RESUME

Here are some other tips:

- Be early.

- Don't bring food or drinks.

- Turn off your phone.

- Shake hands firmly.

- Look people in the eye.

- Sit or stand up straight.

- Listen closely.

- Speak clearly.

- Be polite.

Not all interviews are the same.

People may be warm and friendly.

Others might be more formal.

Many people get nervous.

Take a deep breath.

Show you can **handle pressure**.

Ask about next steps.

Do this before the interview ends.

This shows you want the job.

Make sure to thank them as you leave.

Be gracious.

Write a **thank you note** when you get home.

Not everyone takes this step.

It is a way to stand out.

Keep the note short.

Use the interviewer's name.

Thank them for their time.

Say that you want the job.

Explain why you're right for it.

Find examples online.

Dear Mrs. Doe,

Thank you again for meeting with me last week. I enjoyed getting to learn more about your company.

THANK YOU

Some people send this in the mail.

Others send an email.

Decide which is best.

Send it right away.

Monday	
Tuesday	
Wednesday	
Thursday	✓- One Week since Interview: Follow up with Mr. Andrews from Tech-U
Friday	
Saturday	
Sunday	

Follow-up is important.

Wait about a week.

Contact the person you met with.

Repeat that you want the job.

Ask if they have more questions.

Be patient.

They might not have decided.

You may want to call again later.

But don't be a pest.

That will hurt your chances.

The business might call you.

They may make an offer.

This is the time to talk about details.

They will talk about pay.

Benefits. Work hours.

Are you happy with the offer?

Then accept the job.

You may not like the offer.

That is the time to **negotiate**.

This means give and take.

Ask for what you want.

Know ahead what you'll accept.

Maybe you can't agree.

It's okay to say no.

Be polite either way.

Thank them.

Finding the right job takes time.

It is a process with many steps.

The interview is a big one.

Be ready.

You will find the **right job**.

Then you can really shine.

What happens when Kyle shows up unprepared for an interview? Find out in *Job Ready*. Want to read on?

JUST *flip* THE BOOK!

JOB READY

PJ GRAY

LIFESKILLS IN ACTION

JOB SKILLS

MONEY

Living on a Budget | Road Trip
Opening a Bank Account | The Guitar
Managing Credit | High Cost
Using Coupons | Get the Deal
Planning to Save | Something Big

LIVING

Smart Grocery Shopping | Shop Smart
Doing Household Chores | Keep It Clean
Finding a Place to Live | A Place of Our Own
Moving In | Pack Up
Cooking Your Own Meals | Dinner Is Served

JOB

Preparing a Resume | Not Her Job
Finding a Job | Dream Jobs
Job Interview Basics| Job Ready
How to Act Right on the Job| Choices
Employee Rights| Not So Sweet

SADDLEBACK
EDUCATIONAL PUBLISHING
www.sdlback.com

Copyright © 2017 by Saddleback Educational Publishing. All rights reserved. No part of this book may be reproduced in any form or by any means, electronic or mechanical, including photocopying, recording, scanning, or by any information storage and retrieval system, without the written permission of the publisher. SADDLEBACK EDUCATIONAL PUBLISHING and any associated logos are trademarks and/or registered trademarks of Saddleback Educational Publishing.

ISBN: 978-1-68021-410-9
eBook: 978-1-63078-811-7

Printed in Malaysia

24 23 22 21 20   3 4 5 6 7

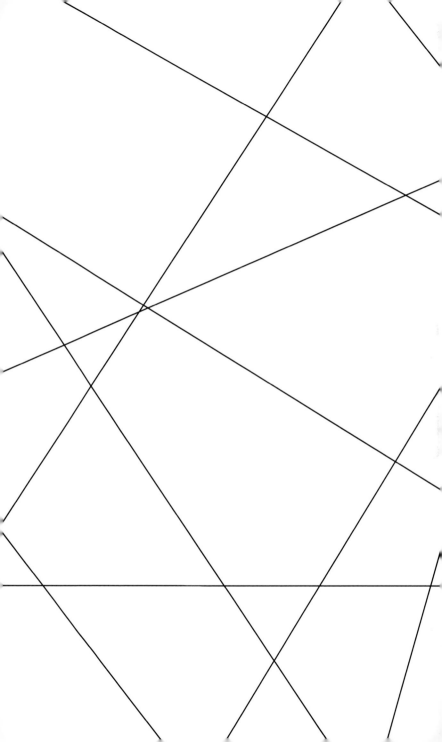

Nate is the manager at a clothing store. He takes college classes too. His goal is to work with computers. People say he is a responsible young man.

Kyle is Nate's younger brother. He just turned 16 and got his driver's license.

Kyle doesn't have a car of his own. He could drive his mom's old car. But it needs new tires. He doesn't have the money to buy them.

It's time to get a job, Kyle decides. With the money, he can buy new tires. He could buy gas too. Then he can have fun with his friends.

Kyle wants to work at the cell phone store. His phone is one of his favorite things. He never leaves home without it. Even better, one of his friends works at the store.

That day, Kyle fills out an application online.

A woman from the store calls the next day.
"I'd like to set up an interview," she tells Kyle.

"Cool," Kyle replies.

"How about Monday after school? Does
4:00 work for you?"

"Yep," Kyle says.

"Very good. I look forward to meeting you, Kyle," the woman says.

"Same," Kyle says. He hangs up the phone quickly.

Kyle is happy to get the interview. He decides not to tell anyone. He will surprise them all when he gets the job.

Monday comes. Kyle is ready for his interview. He wears a new T-shirt. It has the name of his favorite band on it. He makes sure his jeans are clean. He looks cool.

Kyle walks into the store. He goes up to the counter. "Hi, I'm supposed to talk with a lady about a job."

"Are you Kyle?" the boy at the counter asks.

"Yep," Kyle replies.

"I have some bad news," the boy says. "The manager went home sick. She is very sorry. She said she tried to call you. Your voicemail box was full."

"Yeah, I never check voicemail. I only do texts."

"She wants you to come back next Monday. Same time," the boy says.

"Yeah, I can do that," Kyle says. "See you next week, bro."

Kyle leaves the store. *What a bummer*, he thinks. He really wants the job. Now he will have to wait another week.

Kyle decides to stop by to see his brother. Nate works just down the street.

"Hi Kyle, what are you doing here?" Nate asks.

"I went to a job interview," Kyle says.

"Where?" Nate asks.

"The cell phone store."

"How did it go?" Nate asks.

"It didn't," Kyle says. "The manager was sick. I have to go back next week."

"You went there looking like that?" Nate asks.

Kyle looks down at himself. "What? You don't like this band?"

"Come back to my office."

They sit down in Nate's office. "You need to do your homework," Nate says.

"Homework? This isn't school, dude. I'm trying to get a job."

Nate says, "You need to impress the manager. These clothes aren't going to impress anyone but the girls at school."

"I look good," Kyle says with a grin.

"Maybe for school but not for an interview."

"I don't have nice clothes," Kyle says.

"What did you wear to Ali's wedding?" Ali is Nate and Kyle's older sister.

"I wore that white shirt and blue tie," Kyle says.

"Wear that to the interview."

"That's so fancy," Kyle says.

"That's the whole point. You need to dress up. Look good."

"Whatever."

"And no jeans," Nate says. "Make sure you iron the shirt. It needs to be clean and pressed."

Kyle rolls his eyes.

"When is the last time you shaved?"
Nate asks.

"A few days ago," Kyle says.

Nate knows that Kyle is not ready. He has a lot to learn.

"Let's do some interview practice. I'll be the manager."

Kyle laughs.

"This is no joke," Nate says. "Do you really want this job?"

"I do," Kyle says.

"Okay. Let's start." Nate stands up and holds out his hand.

Kyle reaches out and shakes it.

"That was a weak handshake," Nate says. "Let's try again. And look me in the eye."

They try the handshake again. This time Kyle looks at Nate and smiles.

"Good," Nate says. "Keep the handshake firm. Don't try to break her hand."

Nate asks Kyle to have a seat. "What do you know about our phone company?" he asks.

Kyle doesn't know what to say. "You sell cell phones, right?"

"Do you know the size of our company?"

"No," Kyle says.

"Do you have one of our phones?"

"Yep."

Kyle pulls his phone from his pocket.

"What do you like about it?" Nate asks.

"I don't know," Kyle says. "Lots of things, I guess."

"What do you know about the job?"

"You want a sales person," Kyle says. "Someone to sell your phones."

"Have you ever sold phones before?" Nate asks.

"No."

"What makes you right for this job?"

Kyle stops to think. He begins to sweat.
"I don't know. I like people."

"Have you ever sold anything?"

"No," Kyle says again.

"Why should I hire you?" Nate asks.

"I don't know. I need the money!"

Kyle stands up. He looks upset. "This is dumb. I don't want to do this anymore."

"I'm not trying to upset you," Nate says. "I ask these things when I interview people. You may get asked these same questions. You will do better if you are prepared. Think about how you will answer."

Kyle knows Nate is right. He sits down again. "What can I do?"

"Sell yourself," Nate says.

"What does that mean?"

"Convince her that you are right for the job," Nate says. "Make her want to hire you."

"How?"

"Check out their website. Read about their company. Learn more about their phones. Think about how you can answer her questions," Nate says.

"Cool," Kyle replies.

"And don't talk to her like that. You sound like you're talking with your friends. You have to be professional."

Nate asks Kyle for his resume. Kyle pulls it from his pocket. He unfolds it.

"I've only had one job," Kyle says. "I worked for mom's boss, Mr. Long. I took care of his lawn all summer."

"Did you get paid?" Nate asks.

"Yes," Kyle replies. "I put that on my resume."

"Add Mr. Long's contact information. They may want to talk to him."

Nate puts down the resume. He thinks for a moment.

"Didn't you sell candy at school?" Nate asks.

"Yes," Kyle replies. "For the football team. We sold candy all year."

"And didn't you sell the most?"

"Yes," Kyle says. "I won an award for most sales."

"What about the event at church?"

"I sold tickets," Kyle says. "We raised money for the homeless shelter."

"Who sold the most tickets?" Nate asks.

"I did. Two years in a row."

"Why aren't those things on your resume?"

"I thought resumes only listed real jobs,"
Kyle says.

Nate smiles. "You have some good skills.
And more sales experience than you realize."

Kyle jumps from his chair. He grabs his resume from Nate's desk. He turns and runs from the office.

"Kyle," Nate calls. "Where are you going?"

"I've got a lot of homework to do!" Kyle turns and runs out of the store.

Nate smiles. His brother is growing up. He might be able to get the job after all.

Interviews are an important step in getting a job. Want to learn how to get ready?

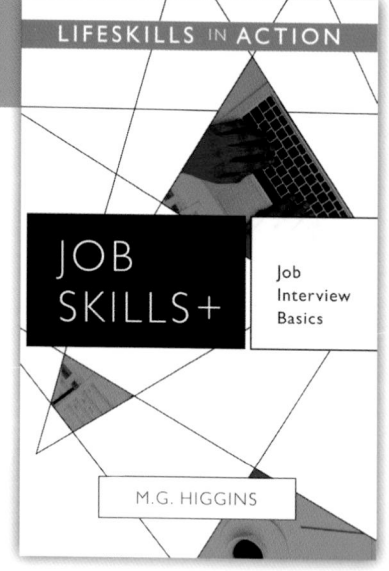

LIFESKILLS IN ACTION

JOB SKILLS+

Job Interview Basics

M.G. HIGGINS

JUST *flip* THE BOOK!